SHEARSMAN
127 & 128

SPRING 2021

FORTIETH ANNIVERSARY ISSUE

EDITOR
TONY FRAZER

Shearsman magazine is published in the United Kingdom by
Shearsman Books Ltd
P.O. Box 4239
Swindon   SN3 9FL

Registered office: 30–31 St James Place, Mangotsfield, Bristol BS16 9JB
(this address not for correspondence)

www.shearsman.com

ISBN 978-1-84861-764-3
ISSN 0260-8049

This compilation copyright © Shearsman Books Ltd., 2021.
All rights in the works printed here revert to their authors, translators or original copyright-holders after publication. Permissions requests may be directed to *Shearsman*, but they will be forwarded to the copyright-holders.

Subscriptions and single copies

Current subscriptions – covering two double-issues, each around 100 pages in length – cost £17 for delivery to UK addresses, £23 for the rest of Europe (including the Republic of Ireland), £25 for Asia & North America, and £28 for Australia, New Zealand and Singapore. Longer subscriptions may be had for a pro-rata higher payment. Purchasers in North America will find that buying single copies from online retailers in the USA or Canada will be cheaper than subscribing, especially since the drastic price-rises for mail to the USA in mid-2020, and then again in early January 2021. This is because copies of the magazine are printed in the USA to meet orders from online retailers there, and thus avoid the transatlantic mail. Antipodean readers will be able to source the magazine from Australian outlets or from the UK's online Book Depository, which—at the time of writing—was still offering books with free postage anywhere in the world.

Back issues from nº 63 onwards (uniform with this issue) cost £9.95 / $17 through retail outlets. Single copies can be ordered for £9.95 direct from the press, post-free within the U.K., through the Shearsman Books online store, or from bookshops. Issues of the previous pamphlet-style version of the magazine, from nº 1 to nº 62, may be had for £3 each, direct from the press, where copies are still available, but contact us for a quote for a full, or partial, run. The single-copy retail price as of 2020 is £9.95.

Submissions

Shearsman operates a submissions-window system, whereby submissions may only be made during the months of March and September, when selections are made for the October and April issues, respectively. Submissions may be sent by mail or email, but email attachments are only accepted in PDF form. We aim to respond within 3 months of the window's closure, i.e. all who submit *should* hear by the end of June or December, although we do sometimes take a little longer.

This issue has been set in Arno Pro, with titling in Argumentum. The flyleaf is set in Trend Sans, apart from the large number 40, which is in Bank Gothic.

Contents

Virgil	(translated by David Hadbawnik)	5
Mary Leader		17
Anannya Uberoi		22
Carola Luther		25
Linda Black		27
Agnieszka Studzińska		29
David Rushmer		31
Melissa Buckheit		33
Susan Connolly		38
Tamar Yoseloff		40
Robin Fulton Macpherson		42
Claire Crowther		44
Jeremy Hooker		46
Amy Crutchfield		49
David Hackbridge Johnson		53
Jane Frank		55
Petra White		57
Amlanjyoti Goswami		60
Christopher Gutkind		63
Mandy Haggith		65
Norman Jope		67
L Kiew		69
Peter Larkin		71
Olivia McCannon		75
Peter Robinson		77
Maurice Scully		80
Aidan Semmens		82
Lucy Sheerman		85
Hannah Cooper Smithson		87
John Welch		90
Charlotte Baldwin		92
Scott Thurston		94
Kjell Espmark	(translated by Robin Fulton Macpherson)	96
Marta Agudo	(translated by Lawrence Schimel)	101
Kinga Tóth	(translated by Annie Rutherford)	104
Notes on Contributors		107

Virgil

translated by David Hadbawnik

from the *Aeneid*, Book X

[*Turnus has just killed Pallas, son of Aeneas's great ally King Evander. Enraged, Aeneas goes berserk on the field of battle. Juno plots to protect Turnus, while Aeneas searches for him.*]

VI. *"Morere et fratrem ne deserefrater."*

Turnus!

There'll come a day you'll pay just about any price
to see Pallas made whole! And rue
            the spoils you snatched.

But
    Pallas's buddies
        groan and cry
             as they gather round
    and carry the body back
        on his shield.

        O sorrow and honor of you
        who bring him back thus
        to his dad. And the war,
        how it gave you
        and took you all in one day
        though you leave behind
        piles of Rutulian dead!

SO
    it's no false rumor that reaches Aeneas.
        He is dead, the prince.

But the troops hang lightly
above waiting death – time
to go help them.

With the sword he cuts down anyone nearby

    looking, looking

        for you

            Turnus

still dripping fresh blood. Pallas,
    Evander flash before his eyes
        scenes
    of sitting with them at table,
        a foreigner
    yet offered the right hand.

So he snatches four youths. Sons of Sulmo.
And four more raised by Ufens.
Planning to send them to hell
in sacrifice, scatter their captive blood
amidst funeral flames.

From afar he aims a lance at Magus
who cleverly ducks so the weapon shivers
overhead
    and he, Magus
        rushes forward to wrap his arms
    around Aeneas's knees, begging:
"By the ghost of your dad and the hope you place
in Julus, I pray, save my soul for a son, for a father.
My house is great. Hidden inside lie talents of silver
and mounds of gold, finished and raw,
    all mine, now yours.
I'm a tiny part of this scene.
Let me just … wander off stage.
It won't make much difference."

Aeneas responds:
    "Keep the silver you talk of for your sons.
    The commercial side of war: Turnus
    broke all that the moment Pallas died.
    So says the spirit of my father, so
    it seems to Julus, my son."

And he nonchalantly bends to the praying guy's neck
and drives his sword in all the way to the hilt.

Nearby stands Haemonides, priest
to Phoebus and Trivia, his brow
encircled by sacred bands, glowing
in white robe and armor.

Aeneas
        chases him all over the field
            and
        standing over the fallen man
            covers him
        in deep shadow as he
                dies.

Serestus grabs the armor and gives it
to you, King Gradius, as trophy.

Caeculus, descended from Vulcan, and Umbro
get the lines back in order. Bad move.
Aeneas rushes against them.
His sword chops off the left arm of Anxur
and Aeneas tosses it and the shield it still clutches
to the ground (Anxur had opened his mouth
to make some great oath and perhaps
he believed it, was bucking himself up
to survive this battle and achieve
the white hairs of old age)
        THEN
    Tarquitus

crosses his path
            born
of the nymph Dryope and woody Faunus
        a proud guy
            well
even as he offers up a lot of hopeless entreaties
Aeneas cuts his head clean off
and turning from the still-warm body
        sneers
        "Now
                rest in fear.
        Your mother won't dig you a grave.
        Your bones won't find decent burial.
        You'll be fodder for birds of prey
                OR
        tossed in the deep, you
        and your wounds will be
                fish food."

His sword's just starting to heat up.
            Next:

                    Antaeus
                    Lucas
                    Numa
                    Camers
    (guys in the first ranks of Turnus's men)

Behold:
        He tracks down Niphaeus'
            four-horse chariot
                and when
                        the horses see
                        great strides
                        tough demeanor
                    break
            fall back

    toss their master
    and haul the chariot
      to shore.

Brothers Lucagus and Liger
    fly into the middle of things
  on chariot and two white horses
      Liger
    holding the reins
    while Lucagus whirls
    his bare sword.

Aeneas, annoyed
  by their attack
  rushes against them and looms large
    with his spear

  Liger says:
    "These aren't Diomedes' horses
    or Achilles' chariot you see
    on the Phyrgian fields. NOW
    the end of the war and your life
      arrive here on this turf."
  Crazy stuff from Liger.

The hero of Troy doesn't answer
  with words.
      Instead
  he spins a spear at his foe.

LUCAGUS
  leans into the attack
  urging on his team
  while his left foot forward
    tenses for fight
      when
    the spear flies under
    the lowest part of his shield

>   cuts through the left groin
>   throws
>   him from chariot and he's
>   dying
>   there on the plain.

Pious Aeneas gives him a dose of tough medicine now:

> "Lucagus, it's not your horses running scared
> or the shadow of your enemy that toppled
> your car, it's you, leaping down, that
> mucked everything up."

And he reaches out and grabs the reins.

The other brother slides down
hands already up, begging:
> "In your own name and that of the parents
> who gave birth to you, spare this soul, pity my prayer!"

Aeneas:
> "Funny, that's nothing like what you were saying before.
>   DIE
> and don't leave your brother waiting."

VII. *quae sopitos deludunt somnia sensus.*

> And with his sword he opens the man's chest
>   releasing the soul
>   from its hiding spot.

So Aeneas deals out death through the fields.
>   Raging
>   torrent
>   black
>   storm.

Ascanius the boy and the rest of the youths
bust loose from the siege and leave camp.

Meanwhile
    Jupiter talks to Juno:
        "O sister and also dearest spouse,
        as you thought, Venus – and you
        weren't wrong to think so – helps
        the Trojan cause, boosting them
        above and beyond their vivid
        warlike hands and ferocious spirits."

    Juno talks back:
        "Why, most beautiful husband,
        do you bring this up even as I
        tremble under your strict orders?
        If my love still held its former weight
        as once it did and still it should
        you wouldn't deny me this, all-
        powerful, the ability to snatch
        Turnus from battle and keep him
        safe for his father Daunus.
        Let him die now, holy blood
        paid out to Trojans. Yet
        he does get his name from us
        for Pilumnus was his ancestor
        and often his hand brought
        great gifts to your door."

    Briefly, the reply:
        "If you want to save Turnus
        from impending doom – if
        that's what you think I have
        planned for him – by all means
        be my guest while there's
        an opening. But if lurking
        beneath this prayer is
        a deeper design meant to

        change the whole war, well…
        you can forget it."

  Juno, weeping:
        "If only your heart would give
        what your words won't. Now
        an innocent man goes down
        to a vicious fate. Or am I an object
        of fun, just another hysterical woman
        worried about nothing, while you
        have the power to turn this ship
        around!"

And she shoots herself through
    the sky seeking the lines
        of battle between Trojans and Latins.

The goddess makes from an empty cloud
a thin, weak likeness of Aeneas (a sight to behold!)
decked out in Trojan arms, shield and plumes
on his godlike head, breathes strange words
into it, gives it sound without sense and strikes
    the pose of his walk.

They say such ghosts stir after death
or in dreams that fool the sleeping senses.

But the imago jumps up happily before the first line
and shakes up the men with words.
Turnus gets a running start and hurls
a spear at him from a distance
    WHIZ
      the imago
        twists away from it
so Turnus believes Aeneas has turned
and wimped out.
      This injects vain hope
into his tortured soul.
        "What's the hurry, Aeneas?

> Don't give up on your promised bride.
> Come here – I'll give you the land you seek."

He shouts. Brandishes his sword.

But he doesn't realize the wind
is already carrying away his joy.

It happens that, hanging from the edge
of a high cliff, there stands a ladder
leading to the deck of a ship
that King Osinius sailed in from
the shores of Clusium.
It's here the imago of Aeneas
retreats in fright. Turnus follows
flying over the wobbly gangplank.
Scarcely has he reached the prow
when Saturn's daughter cuts loose
the ship and sends it careening
into the open sea.
                Then the imago flies
mingling with a black cloud.

The real AENEAS
                meanwhile
urgently seeks his foe in battle
        nowhere to be found
sends many fools down to meet death
while the wind carries TURNUS
off to the uncharted ocean.

He doesn't understand what's happening
and he's not at all happy to safely run away.
Raises his hands to heaven, looking back:
> "Almighty maker, am I such a horrible asshole
> that you lead me to such a pass and
> make me pay such a price?

Where am I going, where have I been?
What kind of man am I?
Will I ever again see the walls and camp of Laurentium?
What about the men who follow me in arms?
The horror, the horror…
I slip off the edge of death
and now their dying cries catch me
as I escape. What should I do?
What hell's deep enough for me?
Winds, take pity. Slam me
against a reef, on rocks…
Take this ship and toss it
on some African shore
where no Rutulians nor
word of my shame can follow!"

His mind flies here and there.
> *Should I throw myself on this blade*
> *out of sheer disgrace straight through*
> *to the ribs or toss myself in the ocean*
> *and try to swim back to the fight*

Three times he tries both options.
Three times great Juno
envelops the youth and holds him back
out of pity. He slides along
high in the air carried by the breeze
and is lofted to the ancient city
of DAUNUS, his father.

VIII. *Nunc morere.*

But meanwhile Mezentius on orders of Jove
joins the fight and goes after the Teucrians
      prematurely celebrating.

They form up and rush at him, screaming
"Where we go one, we go all"—
and he kills them. Well, not all of them.
But it's like when a cliff pushes out
into the wide sea, exposed
to the angry winds and waves,
bearing the brunt of sky and sea,
just sort of standing there taking it.
    Hebrus.
    Latagus.
    Palmus.

        Evanthes.
        Mimas.

(this last, though buddies with Paris, is left
to die unknown on the Laurentine shore)

And now it's like when a bunch of dogs
chase a wild boar. And the boar's caught
in the net, moaning and raising its back.

Not one of those chasing have the *virtus*
to come any closer. They throw stuff
and shout from a distance. And he,
Mezentius, the boar in this scenario,
leaves off snapping his teeth and casts off
the spears from his back. Just so
they keep away, shouting from afar
and shaking their fists.

There's a guy from the ancient borders
of Corythus, Acron, a Greek.
Mezentius locks on him from a long ways off.
See him wreaking havoc: bright in purple plumes,
the purple of his plighted bride. So now,
it's like when a famished lion catches a whiff
of a nice she-goat or a stag,

and crouches over the kill
with gore-stained mouth. MEZENTIUS
leaps at him – Acron is laid low
and hits the turf heel-first, breathing his last,
bloodying the broken spear.

Next up, Orodes.   But…
please don't think he kills him
by remote control, from a distance,
weapon hurled at his fleeing back.
No way. Mezentius meets him
face to face, man to man, plants
one foot on the dying guy's chest
as he grabs the spent spear and says:
> "Check it out!
> No small part of the war, men–
> big Orodes brought down!"

He, dying:
> "Enjoy it while it lasts, buddy.
> It won't last long. Pretty soon
> you'll lie right beside me
> on the killing field."

Mezentius, with a nasty smile:
> "Now die. Let the divine father
> and king of men worry about me."

And he pulls the spear from the corpse.

It's a hard rest and metallic sleep that press down
the eyes of Orodes, whose lights shift
to eternal night.

The killing continues.

Mary Leader

Extant

Max Steinberg was born, family lore
had it, on the 4th of July. The year,
by contrast, was known for sure: 1905.

Last I heard, they threw him a big party
in Miami Beach. A hundred years
and counting – counting, it turned out,

to 103. It's a snap from my comfy chair
to google stats like this. Now that
I am old and gray, very old, and gray entirely....

Sorry. Already, I've digressed.
When I was merely late-middle-aged,
not long after Rose died, I 'penned' – I used to

use words like that – "How is Max doing?"
"Pretty well," answered the early-middle-aged
grandchild, continuing, "I asked him

if there were any activities at the synagogue
he might enjoy. He replied that at his age,
he has no desire or need for friends.

I understand. What's he going to do?
Play cards with other old men?"
Before I ever even heard of that family –

in, for me, a different time and place, namely
when I was at Brandeis, I knew a Bulgarian
who pronounced "category" with the same rhythm

as "discovery" – in other words, the same
rhythm in which my British editor, or any
Briton for that matter, would pronounce

"contrÓversy" – "catÉgory" – which I prefer.
I, not the early-middle-aged person at Brandeis –
rather I, the late-middle-aged person engaged

in asking 'how-is-Max-doing' – thought a lot
about the catégory of Found Poetry.
I had been visiting my own dead four

grandparents, researching card games circa 1955 –
mid-century modern! Design Within Reach™ –
specifically, a Parker-Brothers card-game

called Rook. I was taking notes.
I did, quite recently, write about that game.
You can find the piece, if you want to.

Look in my back bedroom for a black springback
binder labeled with white vinyl letters
THE DISTAFF SIDE except that the letters

are Helvetica, not Times New Roman.
In the alternative, you can travel
to Shrivenham, Oxfordshire, and inquire

therein for my British editor. Anyone
will know which house. If you're not
planning to be in the UK anytime soon,

you may find Part I and Part II of the poem
by going online and ordering a magazine
called *Shearsman*, back issue 123 and 124.

I don't know what I think about that poem's
Part III. It displays a bunch of material
in the found-poetry catégory, derived

from an experimental form of Solitaire –
did you know that in England, Solitaire
is called Patience? – I played with an antique

deck of the card game, "Authors." I sent
to my editor all three parts in a word docx.
He sheared off Part III and kept Parts I and II:

'How Catholics, who do believe in it, play cards';
'How Methodists, who don't believe in it, play cards."
I still go back and forth as to Part III:

'Permissible for all: Old Maid, Go Fish, Authors.'
After all, I have every reason to trust
my Editor's taste! Then again, that Part,

which is, probably, too long at two pages –
I mean, it does drag – I mean, no reader
is going to get that this is the piece wherein

I tell my mother, long since passed over,
that I love her and love her poems and would,
if I had the power, cause them to be in the world

instead of in a green-paisley three-ring binder
in my back bedroom. MEMENTO MORI . . . .
It's been decades since I could lay my hands

on worksheets or drafts of any particular
poem of mine, among them, distantly, some written
during the years when I thought maybe, maybe,

I could win the love of the person who responded
'pretty-well' and so on and so forth. I tried both
traditions: faith and good works. Neither did.

I tried to create intimacy without propinquity,
crafting letters to include, say, a widowered
grandfather. It was never, as they say, on the cards.

But I get it. I was desperate to attract
one descended from emblematic names:
Max and Rose, then Sherman and Bernice.

It could as well have been Morris and Esther,
Sam and Enid, Kent and Deborah. Are there
any activities at the synagogue you might enjoy?

I have arranged all this, clearly I have.
I am alone. I have before my cataracted eyes
at the moment a chunk of notebook that somehow

made it onto my hard drive. Season, after
season, after season – there – it has lain – unseen.
Laptop upon laptop, Mac this, Mac that.

And now – EUREKA – I can read – VERBATIM –
the bit of dialogue recorded in stanzas 5–7 above,
and abutting that, a possibly jejune question –

"lucky or unlucky?" – about the one in a generation
who outlives all of his or her peers. MEMENTO MEI....
Frequently I fail in the gratitude catégory.

And shame on me for it. But thank you, for this
page of pixels, page of light, trimmed with miniature
icons and bordered by a ruler and sign-posting

potential: File, Edit, View, Insert....
I just this minute heard, as I do most days,
a mockingbird in the japon holly tree beyond

my open garage door. I am old. I am slow.
I am grateful, though, that I kept myself
busy transcribing stuff when I was in one

long process of breaking my heart, one
of several. For lo – a found poem – a vestige,
rendered by vicissitude, and by recognition,

a whole. It starts in medias res, the res being,
evidently, a booklet or brochure of some kind
that came with the game of Rook to explain

the rules for playing it, in sundry variations,
The echo: What's he going to do? Play cards
with other old men? The rest of the page:

. . . four cards of the same number.
The player who manages to do so quietly
puts his cards down, and folds his hands

in his lap. As soon as any other player
notes that one player has completed
a set of four cards, he quietly lays down

his cards, folding his hands in his lap.
The player who first gets four cards of one
kind is the WINNER OF THE GAME.

The very last Player to fold his hands
must run around the table three times
calling "I am slow, I am slow."

Anannya Uberoi

the river continuum concept

once upon a time
we were riverine

our skins were streaked in narrow runnels that
ran to *fains-la-folie*
our faces stirred in rhymes of
ripped currents
our breaths whorled against
      each other

our milked words were
watermarked upon our
rigged thighs

we had crosscurrents in our blood cracks
they shapeshifted to form our curved backs
and flowing bellies

our shallow mouths were swamped with slurry.

do you remember

ursa curving in on our paths
where we banked our ferries
and rowed upstream with bare hands

the jelled glacier
was all
salt and rock ice.

*

From the Flower Girl

The wedding street after them—
shrouded in white, cigar smoke,
smoked eyes, leather suits,
birds of confusion, languor,
and warm eyes.
Behind them, a dark horse,
a buried bed, an antique altar,
branching in its hide, quaint canopy,
and light-crossed, barefoot flowers.
Around, a white-feather
sat in an opulent cage, fair flutes
and the passage of whispers.

The road ahead—
soft heeled, a swirling queen
of conceived dawn and drifted cheer.
For her, the sound of the wind
is wood play and damned dreams
are but brambles scythed and dragged
with the cap of the heel.

From the Room in Strasbourg

In a carceral space
the rain, thumping, becomes
an object of dissonance

the diaphanous lamp
at the end of the street bokehs
like a stain of oil on unlined paper

a boat on the water cracks apart into
umbra, penumbra, antumbra

the bells ring and the Strasbourg clock
places her hands on your eyes
the moon buoys up

you study the geography
of a fenceless landscape
half-timbered houses
garlanded bridges
crossroads

the sidewalk wraps itself
around coffin-sized bars
but you turn away
from apparitions with

trembling cups through
intimate windows
for the night

hollow stars above balconies
dim into tree-shaded vagrants
heading home.

Carola Luther

What if not you, it were me

walking down the corridor past all the doors, the doors shut
as faces deeply asleep are shut, like care homes in the night,
lit, drugged by the light, washed out, snuffed out by flat quiet light
as if morning could never come again, which it won't, not the same,
not quite the same as this one morning in my mind, cool and pale
and calm, the sky so high that the fine pencil lines of pink resound
with the high strung silence, its beauty a mesosphere of silence
above its own dawn grass, strange and covered with dew, white
in the way moonlight on grass can be white, colourless and other
and holding its breath, as if breathing would be a path, the trace
of a ghost, a progress of footprints appearing through mist, or one
by one, green, wet, bending the grass and unpeeling themselves,
heel, toe, heel, black as the holes on water.

Who wouldn't want to be the walker that first walked across this
expanse, but before I could reach the poplar tree in the garden
all those years ago, it occurred to me that perhaps I was spoiling my own
immense morning. Why would I remember this? Is it thinking of you
confined within a well-walked, strip-lit corridor, searching for a view, a door,
the one amongst many, shut, brown doors recognised to be distinctive,
a low anxiety settled in your chest, or is it in my chest, that this may be
the passage in which we all get lost, it won't ever end, or suddenly
it will end, so the only place to go is onward, towards that lapping
glare of light that seems to smear out everything ahead, the light
lapping like a lake on this corridor-floor, the shore of an implacable
lake just a few steps in front, always in front, and taking me forward,
leaving no footprints, these, my baffled, slippered feet.

What we know

The horses have gone, and come, and gone.
On this farm they bloomed
brief as arums.

We laid our foreheads against their flanks
and breathed in the beginnings of ourselves
haysweet and saltsweat
and the afternoon smell of hot wood.

Our old man reported
that what had returned to him
was the shape of horses
forming through mist.
They had stood there like nurses
waiting for stretchers coming in from the fields.

He said as he passed they forgave him.
They forgave us all he said.
They lowered their lordly muzzles
and breathed
and now he could forgive us also.

For what? I asked. But these days I wonder
if the possibility of horses is almost
extinct in us.
Through all the poison
and cleanliness
it is hard to be calm.

Linda Black

If you think it

Too abstract, place these images at random throughout (above or below): coppers, stained-glass, lubricant, muslin, iron-filings, tragedy:

Clod, toothpick, hair-slide, haberdashery (choose from many), rent, slipper-socks, railway line:

Shoe polish (recall that tin of ox-blood, its smooth surface, those paralysed flies, the sunken in wedding-cake man), ticket, paper-clip, mizzle:

Farmer Mizzlethorpe is missing three sheep. He is saying it's an ogre.

I am holding a paintbrush

Looking through a window with no glass at a display of woollen garments. Oh dear, I've touched one with the tip and the lady in the shop can't quite wipe off the (white) paint. You'll need white spirit, I say. Judy agrees. Judy's looking for Val on his motorbike. She'll ride pillion (never!) – I'll get the train home. My shoe lace is undone – two pairs, too complicated. Could she please tie it? The worst bit is the queue along the canal. I don't like water. Could you move along please? Can I get past? (Agitation.)

Post script: Next day I find a box containing a birthday card for a six year old boy and a cardboard book, quite a bit of food, an important letter. This gives me a clue. When I finally find the owner, he's stepping along the shore scooping out holes, equidistant. He's an artist then.

Correction: Sand dunes – little mountains – those holes are gouged in rock.

The window is shaking in the wind

In(side) my head I am capable. The cup I create cannot be replicated. Intense reality – fantastical detail. Decades old, almost conical: porcelain, floral patterning (tiny bells), flawed but delicately repaired, widening into a saucer. Neither new nor feasible.

We are on a diversion, knowingly taken, a precious street – bow-windowed emporiums, leaded-lights, blown glass, bullseyes, soothsayers, mortal wares taken/claimed from the dead, curated, displayed *for the cost of a…* bordered by ruins. *Leave the cup and come away with me…*

When first I drew

The latter mind, backwords vision. A mélange – bedlam, tinnitus, malfunction, malefaction. If it were I could be plain, straightforward, explain… to me…

Tell me a story (an old request), a yarn with a through line, neat, in a box, less labyrinthine, happy/hopey ever.

A table to work on. Easel, sharpened pencil (soft), white sheet, canvas, oils, long-handled brush, fine point, magnifying glass, sharp knife, disposable blades, ink tins, palette knife, oil can, hot plate, blankets. Press.

Pending…

Understand me (cat in a hat). Tell me where the worlds came from. How it ended.

Nine short steps, a concrete bowl, associative lapse, kettle, trip-switch, untrained thought.   All at once…

Agnieszka Studzińska

Spring

The magpie hops down from the arms of a fig tree, stopping mid branch in scrutiny of the blackbird's nestling in the curtain length of clematis sprawling against the garage wall. There is no glint to capture his attention as he jumps down further listening to the coiled calls of the blackbird circling her unmade home. From a distance my husband waters plants – though it has rained the night before – quickly dipping the can into the rain-filled barrel. The blackbird, the magpie and the husband move through the sun's pallid signature – a suggestion of permanency arrested in thickets of light. The neighbour has started a bonfire and the smoke of dead things and wood cling to clothes, feathers, seep into frond, corkscrew through the branches of a fig tree like a stairwell leading to the cellar brimming with furnishings concealed from our view.

Area

1

Measurements and weights of this planet are written in beautiful equations.

Earth's mass reads like this:

$M_\oplus = 5.9722 \times 1024 \, kg$

Earth's weight, a suitcase of numbers unfolding in their invisibility.

Ungraspable, these remote lines of formulae like ancestry, this mathematics.

Earth's prevailing blue pulls you down as you sink in its domesticity.

I want to calculate the space of diaspora, that delicate body.

She asks what I means for you? She wants to be that direct.

Her surname has been hidden, only now swells to a surface.

Did you have to change your name? She asks.

Trees recumbent in their sculptural volume of wood, waste and undoing.

A boy climbs the branches of a sycamore with his bow and arrow in position.

2

Perception draws itself into shapes that look like solid structures.

I watch benchmarks on walls and mirrors disappearing.

The map of my body house is folded in an envelope.

I fishtail in the space of that photograph. We become inseparable.

I want to scope sex in this keeping of us like boxes.

I envy the gaze of that animal when it looks beyond you.

Shoes in hallways in exact compositions of distance and place.

I re-learn the field of childhood through his gestures.

I need to be objective about the missing.

This area between us – beryl and breeding, longs to remain.

This is our itinerary: fields, apples, figurines, absence.

David Rushmer

A Book of Skin, or Liberation Through Seeing/Hearing During the Intermediate State

a book of skin.

    There is another

    where it flows.

    to imagine
        a book

    your body

        death
            beyond

            touching
            the disappearance.

            a vanishing

            to say,
            to be observed

            or to butcher
       the eye

II

                sonic
        shores
        of light

       carrying
teeth

   slowly
pushing through you

        skins
        dreaming

                hovering

       bardo form

           collapsing
                  mirrors
        in the hand

III

   When night fell

      she *unfolded*

Melissa Buckheit

Antecedent

With every stone
I do not turn by hand
in the grasses

abutting graves
carved with the characters of the dead
I do not say your name.

I was afraid that to gaze
into your eyes
would be to gaze into my own

the same likeness
of woman who pleases in words;
it is true

I please
you now alone
in my house working

I please myself. I write poems
of the dead and each
dead is a stone

a woman
left, lost or free
so when I don't say *you*

I speak the names
of others:

ghost, ancestor,
reader,
over my shoulder.

I thought to count
them up in a row, the poem
at work

stones
on the tight marker's edge:
Brigid, Brigid Brohedia, Josephine,

Charlotte, Emily, Elizabeth, Virginia
lying among
the grasses, mottled

with clean dirt.
I wrote to please,

to travel far,
to speak these tongues
you taught me.

I left in fear
your stone would be mine
but you can't deny

the living or the dead.
I left to return
as we all do,

on Earth,
Barbara

A Metageography

Not far from loss is home,

                            and the line that runs along
        breaks

in a breath. As a child carries

what is soft in their hand to all places because they feel themselves

        in it, the cloth.

                They know.

So we crowd near a map, gazing in desire.

                      We draw it up,

we build ourselves on causeways and land,

                    we believe.   We long,

we bang our heads against walls that separate, in loneliness

    we thrash in our bedclothes, we cry

out, we weep.

                    There is earth beneath our knees and the stillness of a bird

        in song.

                  The window breaks with its sheer blue and ripple,

like a sheet of ocean waves

                        as we gaze behind ourselves at a receding coast.

          We know it from any boat

or aeroplane

        or on foot.

            How unknown are we, or known,

to anyone, really.

        Longing pulled through genes or memory

to death.
      Body.
            As if this were a geography we could follow

to a real place:
            the green paper a grassy land beneath our feet,

blue water and depth found in the shades of ocean and sea—

each small, irregular ring continuing down infinitely:

                    place your hand inside the siphon.

Can you feel the dead? The living?

Autoportraits, Sofonisba Anguissola

Self-Portrait Playing the Spinet, 1556–7
Self-Portrait with Clavichord, 1561
Self-Portrait at the Easel Painting a Devotional Panel, 1556
Self-Portrait, 1620s
Self-Portrait at the Clavichord
Self-Portrait, 1561
Bernardino Campi Painting Sofonisba Anguissola, Self-Portrait, late 1560s
Self-Portrait, 1532
Self-Portrait with Jeweled Head Zibellino
Self-Portrait, 1560
Self-Portrait Painting the Virgin, 1556
Self-Portrait Holding a Medallion with the Letter of Her Father's Name, 1550s
Self-Portrait Playing the Clavichord, 1556
Self-Portrait with the Clavichord, 1577
Self-Portrait at an Easel
Self-Portrait with Old Woman, 1545

Self-Portrait Playing the Spinet, 1556–7,
Museo e Real Bosco
di Capodimonte, Naples

Susan Connolly

low tide

spectral river

your
backbone
jutting
jagged
your
shallow
water
skeletal
still

i shelter
under
a bridge
watch
sudden
rain
speckle
your
skin

old road

walking
a road
i don't know
until i see
    i do –
Lily brought
me here
long ago
along this
path

what did we
talk about?
i don't know
but
contented
times
long ago
flood
this late June
evening

river-child: for Nicole, Jocsan and Helen

river-child drink fresh water breathe fresh air

```
a    river      helen
  a    child      helen
an    drink      hele
an    fresh      hele
ang    water      hel
ang    breathe      hel
ange    fresh      he
ange    air      he
angel    O    u    r      h
angel    lives      h
angela    l    i    e
angela    in forest
nicole    in river    j
nicole    Protect    j
nicol    the    jo
nicol    forest    jo
nico    protect    joc
nico    the    joc
nic    river    jocs
nic    Stop    jocs
ni    cutting    jocsa
ni    down    jocsa
n    the    jocsan
n    trees    jocsan
```

      Angela
       Murillo
        Bardales
       activist
       mother
       Honduras

Tamar Yoseloff

Field Companions
mesostics after John Cage

(isolation)

Only in caves and houses
do we thrive, in fretting circles
or bubbles, we feed on
what we can forage, plants
and slower creatures;
death arrives for
those who can't adapt.

We dine on mushrooms, pale
flesh flaking on our
lips, their nutty vigour
nourishing our resolve. We will fight
someone shouts, raising a fist
but defeat is easier

bending into wind
like a yew in a graveyard, its roots
clutching bones;
into remembrance we dissolve
for parasites
and nervous violets,
not an end
just another cycle.

(magic)

Alice placed
a golden teacher on my tongue
and we drifted outside to find ghosts
diving through trees,
like clouds, but with skeletons. The air was
a room we could enter. Everything
had edges.

There was a line I kept reciting about
coffins and keyholes, the more I said it
the more I wanted both.
Alice said once you arrived you had to stay;
we were in a garden in Paris –

I don't know how we got there, how we returned
but suddenly it was morning

and everything was grey. For years after
the ghosts materialised,
mostly when I was empty.
They'd appear when night was
at its blackest, in the hinge
between night and day; they'd come
to tell me that death is like
a river you ease yourself into,
after the first terrible plunge

it's fine, almost like being
alive, except you've abandoned
your body –
it has no purpose anymore,
its ponderous limbs and vexing organs
gone – and you're reduced to vapour,
a pure wind.

Robin Fulton Macpherson

South-Westerlies Reach Us

    1

Rain has arrived on our windows.
It doesn't know it's in Norway.
It doesn't seem to remember
drenching peat around Forsinard,
swelling the trickling head-waters
at the top of Kildonan Strath,
evaporating off gravestones
where names like Macpherson don't budge.

    2

In the long hours before hitting
cliffs here gales have had things their way,
churning the waves without looking,
blind to both daylight and darkness,
not noticing, making nothing
of the 30-gram storm petrels
frail commas in a raging text.
The birds know where they're going, get there.

An Outside

I'm sitting outside by a warm wall.
There's much life behind me, between walls.

Cloud-wisps can't be expected to know
why the sky is blue and they are white.

Today's breeze divides into many
nudging *jugendstil* slates and turrets,

tumbling round me like eager children
but they're old, they're millions of years old.

I'm not responsible for their ways.

Barley Field, Kinross

Low cumulus is so blue it's black.
Sycamores are so green they're black too.
The barley field is ripe but pallid,
has taken in more light than it gives out.

If the clouds make noise we don't hear it.
The trees have forgotten to rustle.
An August breeze rasps in the barley
with the persistence of tinnitus.
We'll hear it long after the barley's cut.

Claire Crowther

The Us

I ran downstairs

and said *I've just thought*
we are random
The you and I
The us

Here he said –
       he pushed aside his coffee
       picked up the stapler he'd been using to hold together
       his notes on this and that background to this
       or that experiment –
Here is a set of steel links –
       detaching a line of staples

I felt I was the wall
the molecules of his ordering thought bounced against

He didn't change his speed of speech
And here, he said, *are the staples coming and going*
gripping each other
and going
until

No I said and ran into the kitchen
Too many meanings!
Food is staples
Look: are eggs random?

Oh I'm going to work on a paper he said
And passing me by as I stood at the fridge door
he said, and hardly stopped to say it:

Random interactions of molecules
led to increasingly complex molecules

They became more and more complex
until they could start to replicate

Then order in the universe increased tremendously
until love became an evolutionary principle

I ran upstairs

Tropes Rising

Will you leave your troping and let me pass. —Dryden, 1678, *Kind Keeper*

Don't look it up but surely the trope is rising
to catch us with its cocaine lines. Amine tropine.

Images go among good words like bugs that kill
or any old lies. This makes me trophesic: ill

with a free verse block. Trophonius had a cave.
Seekers who explored that hole never smiled again.

We can't rescue the garden from creeping sonnets
or leaves that look like shields, or flowers like helmets.

But who would not applaud my onward tramp of troops?
Poems want their trophies. Like children, they writhe through

such spoiling, texting cross cats and hearts, blips to rouse
poets: must malign tropes be cut? Get up, good verse,

now you are infected, stagger on till I find
the turn of yearn. Then spring Spring, douse me in rose sky.

Jeremy Hooker

Ghost of an Unwritten Poem

It wasn't one that escaped
    a solitary phantom
appearing and disappearing
among the trees

It was more like the trees themselves
or a thing like a tree
more underground than in the air
    a spirit of all the trees
no spectre but a net
gathering invisible fungal threads
and ghostly entanglements
of roots & leaves & branches

Or else it was a being
with countless eyes of light
    beyond all human vision
though home to the smallest speck
of life.
    Or maybe it will appear
in human form – a mighty hunter
who gathers in all creatures
    bacteria
        lichen
            spore
                bird
                    stag
and histories, stories, myths
wild wood rumours
    tales of ancient plantations
charcoal burners
        Romanies
huntsmen smashing the green

entangled coverts
blood at the roots of an oak

Imagine this thing moving
with creaking limbs
scattering acorns
which grow crossbeams
and wooden navies

It exists and does not exist
in limbo
corpse or embryo
a smoke wisp spiralling
from the compost
of a life   this haunting
may have been a dream
    a ghost
that passed through
like a storm wind
leaving vestiges
of root & branch & twig.

In praise of windows

for Liz Mathews

1.
Look – It begins with dawn,
this apparition
which gradually becomes
a world without walls –
trees, and birds in the trees,
clouds, mountains of cloud,
and all for the gift of glass
that lets the outside enter
and the inside reach out.

2
I begin this in hospital,
hoping, Liz, to respond
to your challenge – someone,
you said, should write a poem
in praise of windows.
So why not me?

3
Think of them, patients,
prisoners, all who are confined:
what a little glass means,
an eye for the eye
to receive light,
as I do here, through
blinds, watching
this apparition
which gradually becomes
a world without walls,
cloud moving along the hills
and a seagull, white in the sun.

Truly, we owe thanks
to the art of the glazier
which lets the outside enter
and the inside reach out
driving back the dark.

Amy Crutchfield

Dora and the Minotaur (1936) ink, pencil and scratching on paper

1 Les Deux Magots

A rook upon the orchard wall, he spies her gloves.
Pink peonies upon black silk, he stares
as she peels them off.
Painted nails, long fingers splayed, she begins the game.
The pricks are rhythmic, ever faster, too close too close!
She does not halt.
Later he aches –
her Spanish tongue, her solemn bronze,
the columns where he would.

2 Mougins

A breeze plays with the drape, fingers
its linen folds, lifts them and then, lets them subside,
time and again, as if nothing existed beyond
touch and response.

Beside the open glass her nipples harden.
A living marble, she soothes him
to miniature strokes,
sculpted pebbles,
littoral treasures,
a paper pup,
a bird on a wire –
constant tokens of his heart.

Each day with friends on *la terrasse*,
they dine inside a cage the awning casts.

Forested hills tumble down to the Bay of Cannes.
Jasmine, pine, lolling petunia,
ivy sidling ever higher.
At meals his restless fingers find
fantastic beasts inside bottle tops and paper scraps, napkins and wire.
He tears and twists until he draws them out.

Siestas bring their usual swapping.
August too has its cruelties.
She brushes off the grains that creep
into their sheets.

Somewhere in the sands they find
the horned skull with its blank gaze,
she bids him raise it to his face.

3 Minotaur

In the shadow of Guernica, she fought for him,
like a cat on the studio floor,
Marie-Thérèse defending her claim,
Pablo delighted, refusing to choose.

Devilishly seductive with her disguise
of tears and marvellous hats,
she feeds his appetite for anguish,
the drama they both love,
plays his games,
laced with cruelty.

The sweetest fish are filled with bones,
Greeks say cats cry to watch us eat them –
the way we suck each bony sickle.
And when one tiny piton lodges, in the secret
pink of the gullet –
It will kill us! Until it doesn't. And then like a twin,
on the heels of small respite, appetite is born anew.

The heart knows its way
to places where the rules don't hold,
and desire betrays us, pipes us
into our degradations.
Or is it the abasement we seek

What is there that hunger cannot encompass?
Witness the snake, who will dislocate its own jaw – the impossible stretch –

At the centre of the universe, a forge,
the heat is *insupportable* –
no fire without fuel,
no flame that does not consume.

He paints her acquiescent, beneath
an orange sky,
her thighs like fallen temple columns,
the tangle of her sex atop them,
the rocky earth, acacia.
With all of love's brutality
he takes her.

4 Museum

At the Bar Catalan
she sees the twin birds swoop,
watches him stride
toward Françoise,
bearing a bowl of hearts.

What is a goddess when she's forgotten?
First the plinth and then the doormat.
There are not enough museums
for all we once believed in.

Each day she starts
a life after, but not without –

boxes beneath the bed, each drawer, each shelf –
love notes, photos, fragments, jewels,
sketch books, pebbles, oils, nudes
143 lots – *objets d'art, de douleur, de perte.*
Love ends when perspective returns.
Without sight lines, there is no
vanishing point.

A tapered finger against her cheek
bears the oval portrait ring – loose
after fifty years. She hears again the way,
swathed in his Spanish "s"
the sound became
"*Cérisses?*"

David Hackbridge Johnson

Broken Consort I

Wood the base of rot the useless limb heeds the dying horn
honest concord the strained breath hence of the pricked thorns
cordon notches mark the divisions the frets running sores
connotes the future of smoking guns kinetic over stones.

Broken moon shortening to crumbs coughed by pale
trees the mulch bark good ribs fountain of the speared
blooded onto ravaged homes the shortening breath in tow
stones set the tones onset of torrents the snatch life drained.

Omen hoots a sooth owl such unshorn the slackened mouth
chained boots boost whether the gift of sacking amounted to succour
mined the blasting of bones corn-fed the eyes of pecked by crows
where minced the sinew by the sword an oak propped.

Consort thine thoughts brought the fine inlay of pearl
he tombs his beginning by the rasped breastplate innards
the tenor holds good for a plainsong bespeaks the uncouth sombre
green limbs hereabout a crumhorn for a splint reed lament.

Here lies William Lawes

Broken Consort II

The chill of stripped bark
consolation soothes him by soft division
wither lines of crow song in canon.

Too soon solemnness a low owl
by the killing bank broken
a broken consort of sighs.

Pavan the insect march
that flesh woeful the raised axe
a riot sonnet of rich meal.

Oath of allegiance mulch
by the leaf mould cortège
aloft by mandibles the heart.

Hoe-in the months go by
blood stain at the root where laid
has ash at the brow swanlike the lilt.

Almayne away thy cares
is far from the sweet-toned viol
now the bud hides where the eye died.

i.m. William Lawes

Jane Frank

Backyard Anamorphosis

We each have a Lawrence Tree
Don't we? When we first ask which
Side is up? The sky standing on its
Head. We hold the trunk, both arms
Tight around it to protect a dream.
Keep it planted. In my case, a gum
Not a ponderosa pine. White trunk
Dappled grey-pink. Arboreal witness,
Leaf litter intermingled with my own
Shed skin. An infinite atmosphere
That same shade – astronomic, on-
Rushing. A sense of the garden as
Blackened moonscape. The younger
Eucalypt sibling silent, thin, no nest.
Fire pit still smoking. Frill lizards lying
Still below red-dusted rocks. A branch
Octopus spreading arms, breathing
Rootedness. Handfuls of grass: now
And evermore reacquainting them-
Selves and after a rush of acid green
Swirls, star faces diving gracefully
From their frame, eyes heavy, a slow
Placid circling, retreat. Pale chambray-
Remembered day canvas. Ordinariness.
Sleep.

Micro Chapters

> *Our nature lies in movement;*
> *complete calm is death*
> —Blaise Pascal

You walk back and forth between the table and the window: short stories in footsteps. Shifts and twists in angles of light on carpet moon penumbras, the colours in the garden thin, tame. You miss the platinum haze of the road north, the fuchsia ecstasy of the island. Roads you remember as threads of imagination before the world got sick, the interlocking sonder of red roofs. Now there is only you and a faint sulphur moon above a brick wall. Paintings have become your memories: figures from mythology in a bush setting or family on a picnic? Patchworks of local colour or decoupaged photographs of people you once knew? Years concertinaed. Cups of green tea are bottomless wells of imagery. The room is warm: one season all year. You remember tiny scales vibrating over a surface of modulated blue, red and orange in Casa Battlo when you hold the model in your hand and see skin magnified: yours. Each cell a micro chapter. A slowing pulse. Tablecloth squares: major and minor keys. You walk your dog around the block: letter box countries. Easy to imagine an ant's life. You can't visualise what's beyond the electric strangeness of the main road. Home: light a candle. Walk to the window: voyage in kitchen reflections, then you journey back.

Petra White

from Persephone at 40

That girl, Eurydice,
sprouting innocence like I once did, if I ever did,
hobbling grandly on her snake-gashed foot.

Poor girl, poor girl! I let him come for her, this Orpheus
who loved her, who thought
hell's whimsical fangs would gently open.

Just before they set off,
on their journey through spidery trees,
spindly bridges over air,

she turned and looked at me, half-pitying
with her golden-green eyes, her girlish smile,
her face in the dun light like a mirror.

And if I hoped to see myself, I was mistaken –
only when she returned, staggering alone
down the crumbling steep steps,

here where nothing can change,
a desert of world behind her,
did something in me smile.

Grief

Time never healed a single wound,
its darkening woods are fed by wounds.
So grief says, with her usual pride.
Only the soul with holes hammered by grief
can float or swim the human sea.
Grief says these things as if they are true.
Grief the key passage through time, her tall ships
sail neither North nor South but into the blinding sun.
The golden life slips from her grasp,
the one in which nothing is lost.
Joy parts the curtain,
she looks in on two lovers lying in bed –
bodies a little overweight, smiles long-familiar –
their radiant souls riddled with holes.

The Young Bloke

The quiet silver water hides his troubled expression,
his flights of wild terror that belong to air and earth.
Down there, unreachable, his pure serene and darkest self –
laid out like a scene that never changes,
a distant valley where his gaze alone will travel.
He does not pour himself through the delicate skin of water –
willingly drowning his own shaking self. He leans forward
instead to gather it up with his cupped hands,
and draw from the cool image, warm flesh.
To father it, as if fatherhood
were as simple as the laying on of hands.
And this creature almost smiling at him...
He lets himself fall backwards through darkness,
the back of his lonely head thudding the grass.

Melbourne

Winter, when the heart makes a cave of itself.
My friends indoors and police roaming the stripped streets
on grey mottled horses.
What is it to love a city where unpeopled trams
squeak like hungry ghosts
and I am far away in another season.
The terror of breath! Of ourselves, driven into walls.
What is it to love a city like loving a wound.
Cold, crisp magnolia trees are flowering
wattle is bursting along roads out of the city
where nobody travels. What a strange love for a city
memorised like a dangerous poem
held in the cave of the heart.

Amlanjyoti Goswami

Salt

After the sugar high, the salt low.
Sodium. Na.
Pinch on plate, pink at sea,
What breaks down food

Makes it energy, makes us run.
A grimy lump left by waves,
Potassium and phosphorus
Worlds last seen in a chemistry lab.

Hard to connect – mood swings
Loss of direction, aches of soul and sole,
With this pinch of earth
And all that's in it.

But if we need someone to blame
There it is, glistening in kitchen dark,
Cat pawing for the moon.
Elan vital, marching like Gandhi.

Or simply, pepper's companion,
Sticking on tongue and wound.
Letting the tongue rip circles across lip
Tingling down spine, a perfect arc

To the curve of arm. That too, salt.
Your eyes stream, for no cause
Unable to find trace of pain.
Rain carries it too.

Gorge it, slurp the remains of day.
Mix it with the day's earnings, all its trouble.
Drench your hopes in it
Be one with it, earth water and sky

It is all, finally, salt.
This loam and substance.
The boy next door.
And where we will all go next.

But while thoughts of sugar occupy,
It is salt that wins in the end, sneaking from behind
This sweltering race,
A leaking craft on turbulent sea, the waves crashing.

Lick it, feel it, let it go
Down the gullet, the tired bone,
Your only companion –
This mulch and liquid and mettle

This mariner's thirst
This shaking sand timer on the table.

Breakfast at the Table

He dug his teeth into the fine red
Particles of the clay pitcher
Cut meticulous with the knife
Till the tiny red piece with jagged edge
Ground with canine and molar
To a red dust when sprinkled on
The poached egg for breakfast
Reminded him of childhood,
The fire of red earth scrambling among ants and dreams
That finally came true for one day he did
Put on a silken grey suit and went further than
All his ancestors with a red tie and hint of cologne
Early morning the first to rise and fresh for the next
Deal at the fancy hotel he was staying in
Where the cutlery clinked and Mozart rooted from the
Invisible speakers on the walls.
But if he were asked about it he would hide
The remains of the piece back into the warm folds of his pocket
Where he kept the room key one of those smart
Biometric keys you just tap to enter
The world of childhood he carried with him
A dream just born and this little secret of red clay
Forbidden forever was all he was left with from those days
Since no one was left anymore but memories are touchstones
Of what lingered in his tongue in his being and a little
Crunched between his teeth like a wafer as he dug
Into the splash of sun and cut one more slice of his life.

Christopher Gutkind

Digits After Orph 1:14—1:17

Learnt to move in the net like fish or fruit games,
caught languages of away as summer from winter
once. Even soft-spoke declare something in the in,
sharing its shops of joining unflesh. Losing Earth.
The dead ramble here and me halfy, screeny still.
Friend can be Shakespeare Marx Mohamed. Also
Jesus Hitler or. We talk 2.0, look for 3s. Someones
operate them, let from words dreams boardroom,
made them move from head. Do they know? Do I?
They'll have a body again or I lose ours, be equal.
Will they count aside you, lung'd console'd outers,
early datafeeler, crewing to still-life, netting ends,
unrotting time, desuffery, everying fit/fairground,
then kissing/killing happens in thoughts I bid on.

Go to I'm scanned, tastes leaving your tongue,
purchase of a record of tales of memory: people
held each other fruitly/smell dancing, now I'm
voicerub working/text toucher, please cybe me.
Love my picture. Fuck my film. We can't forget
you made me your territory far away each day.
It unmatters who I am/where you battery later,
you possess me. Clickity, let me turn into you!
It's mine. Loving your screen. Tap my nospace.
Let me show me what I want to be for any ifyou,
what I undevelop from – lots and unlots of me.
Fundcuddle my platform of nokay to inlife you.
Swipe me in your sides of tag, refate dressings.
You be an orange, I a fish, let's unlove like that.

I can be friends unmeeting. You were outernet,
who is that? I gradually spun in ins, so have you,
squaring holes, looking by away, their eye-urls
overlapping, that's how we metcom, it's no luck.
Sub1.0s pointed fingers/laughs. I feel unmeme
of day, even unme, less compete. Do deleted go?
Is there an unworld of dead members caste on?
Will Orph get them for us if we want – and win!
I'm unsure we bodymeet. But our profiles have
and may be okay. They can't help goggling back,
making sure we were. It's hard to go on/be out.
Anything grows in feet.org, fields of whateverie,
scroll-being, personality circuits, type-feelings,
files of sight. I'll die before install/me in anyone.

Between speck sun. What difference to leave
thru netfix or gify winds or. Into my debreathe.
Everything turns fuel/goes out or gets to new.
Wonders and workers in weapons and words –
they change! Friends2.0! Wouldn't it be nice
to swim in stars, new music's been developed,
I'm to be the white code in a Fallujah 9/11 sky,
always dispersing, untiring, unburning, unsad.
One of you could climb me – it's a new sport.
And if you fall you get to fall forever. Blissnet!
Yet to maintain disparity of rich/not is hard!
We heard we were blooders and then jumped
to simpler, more pure, near constants, airlight.
No one realised how tight the spread in here.

Mandy Haggith

Ten Swans on Lochan Saille

The oak on the south shore of the Uidhe is sleeping.
The holly on the north bank, at the top of the crag
watches over everything, vigilant through dark times.
These are dark times.

As we approach, the swans cluster,
glide to the far shallows, observing us.
We clamber across rocks. Mud sucks at our wellies.
The tide is out so we can get to islands not normally reachable.

We find an oar we lost four years ago,
presumed washed out to sea.
Things return. The sea breathes in and out,
thieving and gifting.

It is a sad morning but the old hazel is still
lichen-garlanded and moss-footed.
Already catkins dangle in their hundreds and thousands,
wish rags on a clootie tree, hopeful despite all auguries.

Although it is midwinter we have to believe in spring,
as the hazel does.
Although the tide is out we must have faith it will rise,
as seals do.

Although sadness and fear are present
ten white swans glide over the dark water.

Seal Questions

A monster and his monstress grow green and old
together in a rock crack in a mystery-infested world
that comes into existence
only if you step into it

here beyond the birch fringe of the dwarf forest
where shells fill shelves
and seaweeds are gathered by the sea
and seals question on skerries overlooked by gulls.

It is enough
that they are asked, these seal questions.
Who are you?
What are you doing here?

The futility of self-importance

small waves
roll in from the Atlantic
curve and smash
reach in towards a million mussels
a billion barnacles
on ancient rocks

in a rock pool
no bigger than a soup bowl
a fish, a crab, an anemone,
seven limpets, eight periwinkles
and two blue shrimps
inhabit perfection

all through a lifetime's worrying
small waves
curve and smash
on ancient rocks

Norman Jope

Broken Flowers

Sitting at a trestle-table in a spacious square, we bless the silence that will claim us as we pick at our food. Discarded bouquets are as if smashed to pieces, the flowers a chaos of metallic fragments through which rats cavort. We toast the void with empty glasses and imagine what it would have been like if we'd had names to answer to. Somewhere, in the distance that extends from the harbour to the ice-floes, there are ships whose crews are hopeful but whose holds are full of bulging sacks that have turned to treacherous claws. Nobody can know what it's like to be dead until they've lost the capacity to explain it to the living, so we don't take notes. On the underside of cobbles beneath our feet, there is a world that sleeps for billions of years and is unaware that it does so, like the tardigrades on the Moon that sleep there now invisibly to the absent naked eye. How can consciousness make sense of unconsciousness, and what darkness persists inside each trampled petal? We pick at our food and leave the most delicious morsels until last, as plague-spores drift and dare us, once more, to open our mouths and let them in.

Zeit

The universe sings when it is all alone and we, who try to listen to its song, are lost beneath its layers of darkness. At the bottom of the star-well, we look up. Constellations circle and the black roads between them are too long for thoughts to traverse. We stare out listening as the lights wheel around, indifferent to our concerns, indifferent to a small blue planet of water on which a species of ape becomes an epidemic and burns itself out of its home. It appears, flourishes and vanishes in the time it takes the light to travel from a nearby galaxy and the noise subsides… scuttling creatures take over and persist without any ambition to make their mark, to have statues raised in their memory. And time denotes their presence as it marked the time of humans, measuring out the hubris and the indifference, the utter indifference of the totality to its parts. Another brief flaring, it might think if it were able to do so… something that had a shape, whose epoch had come and gone and was remembered by nothing. For now, however, we can try to listen to the song that is sung and its infinite complexity, knowing that our absence will pass unnoticed and that the song will continue regardless of our absence.

Silent at four o'clock on a summer morning, we watch the constellations fade as dawn sky lightens… feeling them weigh softly on our eyes and nerves. We live for now, abandoning all hope of a life beyond this life, of a day that follows the day.

Anticipating the First Frost

after Alejandra Pizarnik

I look at my hands as I write
and imagine them plated
with its glacial sheen,
exposed on an iron road
where, from time to time,
I blow into them, in vain.
On a snowbound night
three centuries ago,
a naked woman doused
in freezing water
reaches in vain
for her oppressors' torches.
In vain, I reach for her hands.

L Kiew

Behind lines

There are books and wolves are in the books and roaming between the words
wolves roam between the words and are in books and the world is theirs
Rome between the words and there whirrs the books and there are the wolves
words roamed between the books and are the wolves booking the world from Rome
theirs are the books and there are word-wolves and they roam between the worst
the wolves are in the world and in Rome each word whirrs and whirrs
there are wolves and roan words that roam between worlds and whirl the books
the books roam and there are wolves in the words and between the books
there are words and they roam between worlds with their roan and wolf looks
wolves are words and they are in Rome and roam between worlds of books
there are books and loanwords roaming between the worlds in books and Rome alone
in the books the wolves roam and words are in the world and between
the wolves whirl in Rome and there are words for worlds in roan books
there are words and worlds are in the books and wolves roam in Rome

When I said I wanted to be

Rose what I meant was
I wanted to be that girl prettily
poised at the prow of an ocean liner
ship's wake white behind her
arms opened wide
and nobody surprised
at her   embracing the totality

And now?   I know who I am
not cultivated like roses
drooping   in vases
I am rattan   unsplit cane
nothing decorative   brown spines
strong   climbing   with grace

the messages my laptop displays

filth of filth
the window frames

twittering leaves

this needn't be a warning
without any libel

under trees is unearthed shame

ferns furl
while buttercups have convictions

Peter Larkin

Nominate a Tree to What Windows It

Boughs hadn't parted for such givens   pure convex spaces or no lens this micro-adjacent: slight hollow bulge of welcome

One of its calmants is the twitch into light, the slit lacks snatching at sight: rival intentions (co-dimensions) let slip alongside but not through   not even wrapped in tree-content

        less gapes than
        visual gifts (glints),
        its thrift stations
        light ties into light
        without cruising,
        implicit beam
        gazes past the dry
        midst of branch
        inadvertency
        a stretched fanlight
        is tree transparency,
        no partial vent

Slits don't sip at hovering boughs   their neutral grace is towards/beyond finding what had opened   least valve in the quiescence of a veering gate

At this slit silhouette any macro-canopy is rare, even in emergent leaf

        the slot across tree-
        crown is multi-
        directional, any
        perspective stars
        in it   is it a
        structural failing or
        a host (guest) space?

2

What could have cut into a tree to make it slit this way?   nothing renders it so undamaged, these pristine, virtual shafts   tree-worlding which enamours it to stand, minutely window-wide

Vertical stripes are an opaque premise here   what slits scarcely traffics the light   any passaging can only be means of a contingent unstirring   where a trunk torques, windows do flutter but without cluster

> how a tree prevents
> smudge are the slits
> of it   a window without
> walls, how each is
> peripherally set
> barest interval
> will window a
> horizon to horizon
> natural slits the crests
> of upper tree replicate
> how soil sees its way
> through the roots

Slit a tree's length, skip a tree's breadth   light parsing so lightly its surplus laterals   less a process than barrelless recess   incompleteness defers to a least culmination

> an apprising space, balder
> than any entrance
> a slit doesn't quite
> shine on itself   being
> no sort of rift it
> can't filter the wavelength
> of a purely unattributed

3

Are these sightings a tree-through out from attentive distance?   the incentive wildness foreground is leaf not saturating (sandwiching) leaf

Imperfect transmission does have its tree outline, given this linear artifice of reception   so glints an immediate nakedness of the offered

>   real slits even in
>   leaf-flight, what they
>   lift away from,
>   sudden revelations
>   of the non-oblique
>   a slit is every other
>   parallel a tree has,
>   free of the dialectic
>   between root and branch

Plunge into the generosity of tree but wait in silence before its windows then see them, will be seen by what they don't perforate   offered miniscule non-intrusion, emissions

>   a space many more
>   sides than slightly
>   parted boughs   this is
>   tree concession to its
>   horizon admission
>
>   windows to tree-frame,
>   what was promised
>   this glistered unit

Flash pellets coruscating yew until squirted light ferrets its own clarity, tempo of transparency

4

A topography of contingency suddenly opens to a topology's next living astringency: assigns gentler betweens to trees that were never rent   the after-window effect

Gaps between limbs are complicit, slits within trees their illicit referrals: how cleanly a through-to glimpses margins branch media no longer formulate

> at such slender slits
> a tree is not divided
> from itself, still less
> guided by itself
> to horizon goes horizon,
> only at these ex-
> medial windows
> can a horizon
> see its own
> enmeshing

Tree cluster isn't immanent screen but hybrid by window section   each its own unblinking, openness explicitly unmediated whenever context-imminent   passes a light-bulb on without residue

Slots run tightly along vertical or horizontal planes still unwindowed but there a chance slit does cater an unmade concurrence between two unlinkables   common traversable admittance

> its spare fealty
> to horizon sharpens,
> a tree doesn't need
> to slacken profile
> to be no obstacle

A pinhole to a tree is an entire stride of light   the threshold is every green intermediate tenet   simultaneity of there-tree and here-tree across one tree   full gamut on speck for ratifying the lustre

Olivia McCannon

from Z

Letter
surface debris

Dear Editors-of-Creation,

_{The Z within} I send you these archives from your future's past which is your being present in perpetuity.

Filed by agents hume-ingened to harvest intel here you find the trace of who you were and where how what became.

They reconjig your tech, mutate your tongues, your concepts, disalign your systems, redesign your misbeliefs and stories, bulletproof but harmless unlike you, and yet

they have no insense kin with matter – magnetics – no pheromones no hormones – lack all roots for speaking entropy – dimension time space place. It's funny how

confusedly they speak your Science. Its case is never closed and they want answers but despite themselves make one unspooling song of love-destruction, synched to Z.

_zI send you these to ask if you will play Z's game. Z has infiltered all the data, left zoa prints on every thought and thing, signed them with Z's names.

Sincerely,

Scroll
squid ink on talipat leaf

0.0000001   Z was born walked six steps forwards and at each step an island appeared in zoa cosmic ocean

0.0001   Z laughed zoa breath was wet and warm zoa spit fell as rain and flourished the plants and trees

0.01   Z shook zoa hair so swarms of insects flew out bright and loud their carapaces shining blue and green

01   Spiders shot out on dragline silk to weave from a pattern re-spooling and never completing

10   Birds hurtled up and out low high to hear and be heard sing and be sung to be the lungs of the sky

100   Z heard how the old earth longed to howl and wept along with its rocks so blood lava salt flowed into lakes

1100   Z went on five journeys met a sick being an old being the bones of a being and a being-becoming

10100   Z existed ∞ in rocks in gases in aquifers ferns in dragonflies in dying stars in plankton

1001000   Wherever Z walked zoa footprints filled with crude oil were dogged by hume time and design

1000100000   Z's auspicious emblem is infinity accommodating any thing orangeslice umbrella goldfish
        daisy snailshell piggybank
        protestbanner
        lithium
        sunlight
        lead

Z   Z   Z   Z   Z
    Z   Z   Z   Z

Peter Robinson

Other Light Effects

> 'die Syntax kreuzigen
> auf einen Lichteffekt?'
> —Ingeborg Bachmann

Pink-streaked, these pallid blue early dawns pierce
through shrivelled leafage stirring
on the courtyard's Lombardy poplars,
illuminating russet remnants
gusted, tumbled over grass.

They reach through our shutters to still lives
surviving with candle, nutcrackers,
and a yellowed *Gazzetta di Parma* that opens
on this Christmas morning.

*

Now Apennine profiles appear at a distance:
backlit, heaped up cloudbanks
give us a momentary stay
as rose-touched Alpine peaks just go
to show the plain's extent –
revealing its prospects like never before;
the firm colours form in bright air.

Still here, long shadows of that winter sun
proffer relief as I'm waiting, absorbed,
somewhere between 12:30 and 1:00.
I'm watching a dog lift its leg to a waste-bin
then lap fountain water and leave,
leave us here in our double dream of home!

*

Knowing only too well it's time we were gone,
as remain is no longer an option,
I'm wanting impossible outcomes, to stay
where holm oaks take us unawares,
their gnarled boughs on an off-white ground,
and brown-tinged, pink camellias
stand up against a mist.

Then from the ridge scree-falls emerge,
a vantage-point as whiteness
becomes this blank cloud-sea.
We're cut off by a Channel in the valley
and laurel too, red-berried holly
are fast while glasses celebrate years,
like that stirring of our poplars' russet leaves…

*

For that was the colour dawn gave to those leaves
here in Emilia, as she would remain,
her co-ops, her partisan memorials
high on street corners, in graveyard or square,
and her promise of underground streams only gone
into hiding, away from inopportune times,
emerging – you'll say –

to disarm blighted distance, despondencies past,
and urge a resistance, mock leave to remain
in the lost air confounding our stay.

Fireproof Depository

Not ten years gone, the sight
of Rembrandt's 1669
Self Portrait at the stair-head,
a bankrupt's battered pride,
would bring him back to mind.

Displayed through a long retirement,
it was going to be my cover,
an image with great concrete structures
in desperate states of disrepair.
They were ones we'd rounded on a beach,
that dome-like rocky coastline
'somewhere in Sicily' or maybe southern Spain –

which is how it would start up once again
in an estuarial, a riverine dreamscape:
on elevated railway journeys
through close-packed heavy industry
we'd shoot past shipping, oily waters,
with all the speed, the overflight
of a sea-level camera towards cloudy night…

Port Sunlight! A lurid yellow dusk
come down behind dad's forehead,
no, that was going to be my cover
(if the copyright holder hadn't asked so much),
its chiaroscuro of gravy-browning
and salad cream from which emerge
his wearied, glaucous, understanding eyes.

He had parked a lifeboat in the drive.
Back home from his pastoral duties,
look, in our kitchen, smiling despite
late illnesses, back pain, fret,
he's drying the dishes; or, see, he's
sighing over his Sunday paper
spread on the living room floor, a quiet
posthumous kind of existence –
surviving in others' memories;
and as if he really hadn't died,
was driving, still, round Merseyside,
if its image hadn't been denied
this was going to be the cover.

That's how I dreamed my father, still alive.

Maurice Scully

Lullaby

In a pool of light
two books used to
prop a third
under the
extended light-cone
of the lamp
in the dark
of a stormy night
in February
near the sea
layer over layer
quiet inside
settling into
work again
cascades
patterns
a neat fit –
grammars expanded –
jelly lichens
that contain
nostoc
a cyanobacteria
instead of
algae ...
that after-rain calm
that spatters
your shed-roof
in the cold
helping your mind along
through the trees
their typo-happy canopies

in sunlight
shimmering
under the hills
over there where
you remember now that
viscosity is
measured in time
in units of
poise.

Aidan Semmens

On the side of the angels

"after Hiroshima it is scarcely possible to write poetry about mushrooms"
—Drew Milne

call me Azrael
angel of death, destroying angel
high above, that silver glinting speck
my symbol, whomsoever
it shall wreak its destruction upon,
a storm of bewilderment
from my hideous wings
in sheer infinite descent
visiting endings on the unsuspecting
delivered from men in cold hats
in distant sheds
cultivators of the ultimate
wonderful death cap

the only sure means of prevention
is to be able to recognise
this highly poisonous fungus
beyond any possibility of doubt
it is not true
that all poisonous species
have a bitter flavour

the sublime atomic spectacle
of permanent catastrophe
masterful negation, impossible songlines lie
in industrial management of hospital detritus
radioactive lesions leaving
waste like the litter of neolithic flint

the most potent is amanitin
which works slowly
and in the pure state forms beautiful
needlelike crystals

Gerontius in joyous mourning for a lost
or possible future
dreams of nuclear weather
as we cheer each launch
in social pacts of denial
repeating the triumphalism
of bomb as utopian spectacle

the second poison is phalloidin
a hexapeptide which acts quickly
in cases of recovery the after-effects
remain often for life, vomiting merely
irritates the stomach to no purpose

'traces of strontium-90 in our teeth
can be used to date our corpses
against the datelines of nuclear testing'

Angel's egg

For Lucy Hamilton

In the egg there is an angel
destined to take its place in architecture
on the high unseen façade of a public building
or the wooden roofwork of an ancient church.

The incubation period for an angel
is longer than the idea of a poem,
longer than for a public virus
that will be born of uncertainty, indecision.

In the egg there is another world,
of a different kind where churches are not needed,
where no one believes in angels,
where everyone tells stories and no one needs to lie.

The incubation period for a world
is longer than the idea of a story,
longer than the dreaming of angels,
longer than anyone's need for words.

In the egg there is the word 'angel',
destined to take its place in the idea of a poem
in the high unseen window of a private space,
born perhaps of too much certainty and decision.

*'Angel's egg' was written to a commission from
the Xu Zhimo Poetry and Arts Festival.*

Lucy Sheerman

from Pine Island

Fulbourn
Tuesday, 19 June

Dearest,

I am thinking of the web we weave in childhood and how it catches, catches, catches. I have scratches to the hands, bruising as I fight with my son. We are battling over my son's desire to escape, as he tries to run from me, again and again, and the opposite one, my wish to contain him. This time neither of us is giving in, or I should say, this time I'm not because it seems the calm it brings is far crueller than the storm of putting boundaries around his fierce wants.

After his school sports day he is in meltdown in spite of the meticulous schedule, the repeated rehearsals of the plan, his own fervent assurances, my promise of tangible rewards, consultation with the experts involved in his care, the painstaking arrangement of the journey starting here, where I found a space to park the car, near to school, far from the house. All these steps have still led us to another scene. He didn't mean to keep his word, that he would go back to the Unit with me.

Each time he tries to run away I stop him. 'I want to go home', he pleads, but that place is unravelling and where we belong is shifting. 'We're not going back there', I say. Neither of us can. In any case, even as the rest of the family head that way along the sunny streets, our home is changing because it must. It's not that he didn't want to be parted from them so much as the knowledge that they went home without him. I don't know if I have the strength to keep on, to make my will stronger than his. It would be so easy just to follow them but, instead, we are going back to the Unit.

'Help me, help me', he screams out to the passers-by as I hold him. But the man who stops to help turns to me not my frantic son. This is not mothering, it's something else, something even harder. Blankness. I may have laughed at the inevitability of this stand-off in a quiet street, I don't remember now. It's not until the following day that the therapist talks about the difference between acts of love and kindness by which he means, in this instance, the way that they sometimes oppose each other.

Yours,

Fulbourn
Wednesday, 20 June

Dearest,

The therapist wants to know who has suffered the most in this family. We both know what he wants me to say. So easy to choose this stuff as suffering, but you can make it something else I suppose. How to translate this rough material that is always shoddy. When I was young, I could give my grandmother any piece of fabric with a description of the garment I wanted. So those are back in are they, she'd say, then take her dressmaker's scissors and 'make it up', however drab, into a new thing.

Am I always turning to daydream or is this the real place? He wants us to remember what we were like at our son's age. The childhood in which threat loomed like a mushroom cloud. The storm and thunder of my father's return each weekend. You think that you ought to have forgotten all this but it happened.

I am unremembering who was lost then, imagining a time where we were the strong ones, carrying our mother on our backs, keeping ourselves afloat as we bobbed along through the hard rain and darkness of those smoke-blackened buildings, the jagged moors. It's as if we might have found anchorage in the idea of being abandoned. If I decide to look back I suppose I cannot choose what my eyes will light upon.

Yours,

Hannah Cooper-Smithson

Ghost Apple

In the orchard, a blue-white shell of ice
hangs on a low branch on a low tree –
it holds everything you know about apples

> [apple, or apple, eple and apful, epli, aeple, aepael, apel, *ab(e)l,
> the root meaning apple, but also a name, Hebhel, meaning both
> 'breath' and 'vanity' and 'murderer' – an apple is an any fruit –
> finger-apples, earth-apples, love-apples, apples of paradise – an
> apple is a man and a woman crouching naked in a garden – Eve
> ate an apple, but so did Adam – it stuck in his throat and calcified
> – the pip of an apple-apple contains cyanide – you would need to
> chew 200 seeds to die by apple – in a fairytale an apple can kill
> with a bite – the apple of the eye is the pit of the iris; it is also the
> one that you love – the apple is both the fruit and the tree and
> the colour – apple is just a shape – apples live in the cheeks of
> children and virgin maids – mad-apple, mayapple, oak-apple, the
> gall of the wasps – *Apple-time is the third Quarter of the Year* – an
> apple is a pome, a *pomme*, a ball, a globe, an orb, a knob, a heart
> – apple is a verb, to swell, become globular, apple-shaped – to
> apple is to gather fir-cones, for the specified purpose of burning
> – *children love apples more than gold* – to be appleless is to be
> without apples]

apple-knowledge leaks from a pinprick
in the apple-case, leaving only blue-white glass,
the suggestion of an apple-shape.

Three Stages of Citric Hybridity

I. Oranges

Oranges, Jeanette says, are not the only fruit — there's also tangerine, satsuma, mandarin, clementine, pomelo, Seville, navel, heirloom, bergamot, bitter, blood — and oranges are also apples of gold and Cézanne painted oranges and apples together on a white cloth and you could never tell them apart — and half an orange, it is said, tastes just as sweet as the whole, and Fred Allen, the absurd one, said that California was a fine place to live if you happened to be an orange — and an orange is a fruit and a blossom and a thing that you can say, and it's also a city and a county and a lake and a park and a river and a creek and a cap and it's also a colour but the fruit came first — before we had oranges we only had yellowred, *geoluread, geolucrog* — and the orange of an orange is actually a carotene the colour of leaves in autumn and the robes of Pomona and the sun in *Impressionist Sunrise* and the fur of the fox and the wings of the oriole and the scales of the koi — and orange was an agent deployed in Vietnam and orange killed the jungles and the forests and orange irradiated all the babies and blossomed cancers in their bloods and orange cleaved their palates and bifurcated their spines and genes and neural tubes — and orange used to begin with an n but now all we have is o — and underneath the peel and the pith of the of the citrus fruit, you will find carpels, membranes, vesicles, pips.

II. Peels

A peel was pole used for shovelling bread, a peel was a gallows, an executioner's stake, because a peal is a clamouring of bells and tongues, it's a begging, a beseeching, a plea for your life –

to be cured, like a salmon in a ceviche marinade, trichloroacetic acid searing into the soft flesh of your face, melting away the dead and dull, all visible consequence of age in the skin –

pared off with a blade, stripped, sliced, diced, boiled in a vat of liquid sugar, and baked into a cake that is wrapped in linens and preserved for a hundred years, waiting for the right wedding, the right bride, the right birth.

III. Pith

from *piþa*, meaning substance — it's the soft, interior tissue — *it's the innermost or central part of a thing* — it's the webbed lining of the rind — it's the keratin-core of a feather and also the core of a horn — it's the vascular stem of a plant that shrivels and dies and leaves only a hollow space — it's the porous sponge-cake layer between the strata of the skull — white and often bitter-tasting — it's the sprung white heart of bread that you tear out with your fist — from *pitte* meaning pit — it's a cavity, a hole, the smallest deepest dark — *some do twine out the pith of the backe with a long wire* — it's the literal and figurative backbone — the core, the nub — it's the mettle, the spine — it's to be of great import — it's a lace, a marrow, a pudding, a ball — *it's the spirit or essence*, the spark of courage that streaks from the belly to the throat — it's a cavity, a marrow, a pudding, a ball — it's a helmet worn in the jungles of war — it's *the innermost or central part of a thing* — it's an act of violence, an insensible severing, a terrible snipping of the spine — *the essential or vital part* —

John Welch

Some of Them

For Carl Rakosi
Sometimes when looking at what I wrote
Back then and thinking, if only such plainness
As this man's here
Who once went silent, before
Being summoned to speech again.

Visiting Hölderlin
'I asked whether I might keep one of these papers covered with his writing'
—*Waiblinger*

A long drawn-out agony of expense,
A moment of exile from the punishing voices,
Such dispersal of wealth among these dishevelled papers.
His visitor records
'When it is intelligible he always speaks
Of suffering, Oedipus and Greece'.

Concluding
A researcher visiting Christopher Middleton's archive in Texas found in there a pair of the poet's shoes. Middleton's poem Without Shoes begins 'One goes lightly / Down ignorant rays…'

Unshod, the dark wood
Being lightly entered
All signs abandoned
The poet's shoes
Have walked him into an archive.

An Aftermath

> – Half of the roof
> Acanthus circle gone and the ceiling
> So absurdly high it took a week to notice it
> —— *Tim Longville*, 'Along Bohemia's Coast'

Along Bohemia's coast make landfall.
Maybe when the weather has eased a little
We'll hunt for them. Yes, gone,
End-stopped lives, a faltering – and me
I'm living in the aftermath already.
Back then a loosened line discovered
Needs I never knew I had, back then
When there was all that time
And always someone whose name went missing.
Until one day
This one came knocking at the door
And here he is, whose book smiles in your hand.

Charlotte Baldwin

The Brontë Sisters at Dinner

On Tuesday nights the sisters eat at Pizza Express.
Their father is invited, but is usually busy reading the Bible.
Branwell is never invited because of the proximity to wine
but sometimes comes anyway, embarrassing everyone
being drunk on a Tuesday in the only restaurant in Haworth.

Anne is a vegan and checks whether the flour
in the ready-made dough is fairtrade.
Emily likes to sit by the window – a small square
of moorland is visible behind the church if she angles
her chair slightly away from her sisters.
Charlotte books the table and mostly pays the bill.
Sometimes she criticises her sister's menu choices:

The American Hot is too hot for Emily!
Why does Anne worry so much about dairy
when all their neighbours are farmers?
Charlotte always has the same thing.
Together they scribble ideas on the branded napkins,
produce vouchers, leave poems about birds
in the silver dish in place of a tip.

Letter to a Long Term Illness

I lived twenty lives as a sorceress before you came,
each of them more impossible than the last.
I watched rivers pick themselves up
and stroppily spill their innards
over new ground at my smallest command.
I conducted rabbit operas, choreographed
a deer ballet of improvised leaps.
I tuned grasshopper orchestras
for their evening performance,
persuaded grass snakes to offer their length
as wires when lightning came
and couldn't reach the hard earth.
I took them all in my twenty strides.
They were nothing in the face of you.

I folded up my lives and ran to escape you
but the hard earth opened to swallow my flight,
stretched me like wire beneath your lightning.
You greyed my young hair and sold it
to the grasshoppers for their bowstrings. Still
it was not enough. I hid below the grassline,
stayed silent while the rabbits sang,
let the deer dance on me until I bloomed with purple bruises.
When you caught my scent on the wind
I begged the rivers to forget their grudges,
roll themselves over me like lovers in their sleep,
crushing the memories of all I had
before you came. Still you wouldn't give up.
The taste of the twenty lives I could yet live
with you in them sits in my mouth like ash.

Scott Thurston

from TERRACES

One leaf never one leaf, the green cloth-bound with browned papers. Going down into a core stretch: give weight, pull, swap. For a comma, a turn, turning to change position for each hand, turning head. Add to the same level of tension: top half not connected to the lower. Your silence got lost in it, beside the floating mountain. Those bleak terraces.

*

Micro-decisions in the moment – attention to what relaxes. We meet the same situation with different qualities in collaboration; our emotional eco-system. When the I fully realises itself, there is a corresponding change in the other, but if I don't speak, you think I am thinking the worst possible thing. The mountains obscured by cloud at the base appear to float. The vines in winter.

*

During the ceremony, the course was physically installed in my body. How to best serve the universe, allow oneself to be held, reconnect with the centre, stay grounded? Movement connects us to what is happening now. Finding one's full height – see the pattern's roots, make a choice to find the new or maintain the old. Breathing first and last. Rite to take up space.

*

Release anger to get past it – the past source of energy. Change our relation, enrol each other in drama, bringing love to what is unloved. My fear fulfils your fear – pure seeing by grace alone. Tell me, does it dignify life?

*

To still believe in a future: is becoming worthy of trust by knowing and owning my own patterns disciplined or compliant? You covet your resources and get upset if I use them and don't replace them. Free energy up by learning the secrets of the past – how to reform the sick institution? Keep the spring clear. To recognise our power, trust our force to give more energy in the meeting without compromise.

*

Sex, life, work, struggle: certainly reaching for mountains. A wisp of expression, cupping a bowl of intention. The Citadel of the Eye of the Heart. Shadow city: how fear and stress start to climb in my body – seek extension, upward release of tension. Standing in my height and strength, integrating the upper and the lower. Crucible of blood: the pain is in the in-between.

Kjell Espmark

translated by Robin Fulton Macpherson

When Music Finds Bartók Again

He's thin as a worn dollar bill.
But his gaze insists: a welder's torch.
It was tough when they took one of the pianos,
cutting earnings spelt "four-handed."
And leukaemia took his very energy.

In a U.S.A. of indifferent backs
he's a five-year namelessness,
a Central European who argued his way here
with his pride and his scuffed luggage
and works for peanuts in some archive.

In his music sheets, exhaustion, nothing more.
Where's the smell of the sun-warmed soil
and the uneven stomping peasant rhythm?
The street racket shreds his nerves –
earplugs don't help.

It's only when he's become almost abstract
that he hears quarter-tones scrabble up from the street.
The incomplete seeks him out
with features still trapped in the stone.

Perhaps simplicity begins in the music
he wrote for little Péter's fingers.
But it must find its way through difficulty.
It's the density of the string quartets
that makes simplicity possible.

The late style remembers all the heaviness:
Goebbels' music-making boots,
the panic of those held back at the border
and Ditta's despondency: a bundle
in a corner of a hospital of hard-of-hearing stone.

Remembers everything but is still transparent.
The long-suffering features of the piano concertos
free themselves more and more from the stone.

Anna Akhmatova's Still in the Queue

This winter morning too
takes the deceitful shape of hope.
The queue of women waiting for news,
exhaling a haze of despair,
stretches ahead to the end of time.
Are there really wickets away up at the front
with bad-tempered calls for patience?

We see day after day dragged to the cellar,
a black-and-blue Monday, a thrashed Easter,
for the shot in the nape called mercy.

She herself is ten years older
than history's blackest century.
The silver willow with its grey light
has far too much to tell.
Chop it down!

Is recognized by a woman with frozen blue lips –
Can you describe this?
I can. Just because my language is forbidden.

But what can be hoped for? That the missing person
will manage to break free of their fate
like a corpse emerging
from the melting ice of the Neva
to come floating into the present?

When a son is snatched away
his photo on the bedside table fades.
His smile becomes more and more uncertain,
his eyes more and more irresolute.

What's left is to rescue the language,
smuggle it through this night of iron
to the possible world after us.

My readers don't yet exist
but they keep me awake till dawn
cajoling for comfort. So habitual
that witnesses agree to lie.
As if my son could step out
of the grief-blackened mirror
and embrace me.

No, poetry's not what you want.
Poetry is clouds of blossom in a blackthorn thicket
that refuses to give up its barbs.

from A Cloud of Witnesses

I was long on my way to exile,
sentenced by Augustus
to lose my life hour by hour.
The ship was already reduced, day by day,
until it scarcely touched the waves.
Only my heart had weight.
It sank like the anchor
on this black coast.
Hurrying clouds wanted to erase my name,
the gibberish around me to silence my language.
But my Epistles demanded to be written –
their splinters of grief shimmering.

§

I, Farinata, saved Florence
with my rhetoric
when the Monteperti victors
wanted to level the city.
What crime can have brought me here to Hell
sentenced to see the future
yet helpless to warn my nearest?
If only I could sharpen my eloquence
thin as a razor edge –
then it could slip out through the gap
between past and future
with words which this time would save the world.

§

When their sails brought them to our island
the white men burned our helpful gods
and the tales that gave us roots
in our ancestors' mumbling humus.
It was an unequal fight for memory.
They scraped our skulls empty
and filled them with their sick story –
one that starts when they nail up
their god on a pair of crossed planks.
I want to get home to our burnt past
to place seeds in the rich ash.

§

These Siberian barracks, a mass grave
we make as comfortable as we can,
have taught me to think with my body.
And I've understood, Nadya,
that just because I've been snatched from you
so you're always near me.
I've even grasped
that only low words
like earwig, sole and Mandelstam
can slip in through the gap
beneath the door to the future.
We must abstain from a claim
to take dictation from God
if we're to produce a text
that moves freely over the ditch
between oblivion and the lilac copse.

Marta Agudo

translated by Lawrence Schimel

Poems from *Historial* (*Case History*)

...for death is nobody. A sudden switching off or bit
    by bit, like the light that dims each afternoon in the
    eyes of the sick.

The patient or the gradual surrender, that wingless flight. And the
    world that moves thanks only to the desire that
    it may dawn the next day. A pathological impulse
    to elude the cadaver we harbour, to cling to
    the granted opportunity.

Only Cernuda knew more than I, only Bosch, only García
    Lorca. Three names and an architect: the memory
    of the Pantheon or the sand suddenly redeemed for
    ten seconds more in the history of the universe.

Yes, a history of the universe told backwards would be less
    deceitful, hypnotic in its beginning, perhaps enduring
    in the first maternal caress.

Yes, a score read backwards and finishing with the key that
    marked our days. Free will then, not
    being prescribed.

Yes, a chimeric sculpture. An unattainable work is equal
    to another that won't let itself be started. The marble or the struggle
    with arm raised against time...

§

In the beginning, the systole. Expansion of neurons, bones.
    Blood structured in rising conjunctions.
    Instinct doesn't involve uncertainties. Only he is the
    pleasure of the rivers, fertility of two hungry carcasses.
    Subjected to the incomplete idea of evolution, the
    seed becomes ulcer, the fish a naked ape, and the enclosure,
    the home of the daring.

It was in principle the diastole. Contraction and sinking,
    the submission of ten truncated phalanxes, the paleness of
    a god soaked up by his own nature. The clamour
    of what's thrown down reclaims its edges and the glass
    enunciates the death of the father by his children.

Order and chaos like siamese twins, reciprocal minutes. To write
    the alternating of the beam and its underside, extract or leak that
    circumscribe the perfect perimeter.

§

Third floor. There, like Orpheus seeking Eurydice, the doors of the "Stroke Ward" open. The stroke or learning that nobody moves by legal imperative, but instead through two hundred million cells in the banquet of health. The shout of those who lack it is heard… the mature woman wiping away the saliva her husband doesn't swallow or bibs to cover the uncertainty of how much more he can endure. The stroke or members which no longer, molten ash, perhaps hand rehabilitated to caress that new microworld of fresh sheets, open perfume, sneakers new as irony. And "please, don't forget me"… Throw the stone and hide the hand… Throw the stone…

§

Five feet seven inches, two or four pounds extra, twenty eight teeth
    and two cavities. Lying down each morning alongside
    life. It's not so much the routine as the tedium of meeting
    the sanguinary rhythm, caboose of cells. Outline
    of some centre, magnetised film of itself that
    rises to fall once more. Camus decreed it.

Breaking ties to avoid hurting, a blind eye turned, rough hands
    that cut or capitol closed with drowsy fool.
    Wind up remaining along among nodules of conscience, with
    neither space nor time now, nor another dimension than that of going,
    little by little (with the changeable pretence) of the fish that doesn't
    breathe), letting yourself slide.

The merit, it is known, is in resisting, but I wasn't born for odysseys.
    Approach this body and you'll smell my decision, perhaps
    the most dignified one. To get rid of my matter without prejudice,
    to dispose of my own surface blindly or not, in
    spoonfuls of bone and bulimia.

Kinga Tóth

translated by Annie Rutherford

Water carrier

brides are for sale in the window
I ask when will it be my turn for a
white dress like that it'll definitely be
but only with trousers or definitely
only with trousers
I could have put a match to that window display
thrown fire at the dress
hot cherry stones under the dress
but the house was over there above the foot of the mountain
still have to go through the woods next to the walls three cloisters
next to them the church too and then another and then
avoid the path to school better take the detour
on the hillside climb in my shoes
the woman carrying water the nuns even a noblewoman
I walk like them I carry the bucket
there is no noise does anyone live here no
movement in the bushes only if commanded only then
will a wee creature run between the bushes
then a car can be heard in the distance
and a young man is walking but
turns back the cloak tears and everything
else no break one thing after another
as he walks the young man asks thinks
is alone but along with me
he hears the other questioner in the bushes
in the next valley and on the other side of the bend
the man with both shoes I carry them
to the top of the hill then there's nothing left to do
and for the first time we take a breath

the noblewoman begins to clap inside me
the nun claps too my long cloak dissolves
the string my shoelace flakes off my dress falls down
the cloth falls from my mouth and then this breath drifts through my
windpipe cools it down let it be harsh leave all that
my way out of it my mother my sisters
I am arrived

Flash gun

when they sat me on the posing stool
and I placed myself behind the dressmaker's doll
I was fixed in pale blue and egg-shaped
but the needle sprang off my skin
and the horse in me began to run
and my toes became redhot
and the streetlight flexed
orangeyellow
little furs ran across my skin
and my hair threw off my hat
my son waved from the back of a sheep
benjamin rose above the aeroplanes
the keyboard toggled between languages
and I landed in lightbulb filaments
I glided through this circuit
from left to right
they might have been Christmas decorations
then the mortar the pestle blazed in my eyes
this is the circle doctor manhattan
this is the point the run-nerves come from
the ones that slide into the camera lenses
when the mortar covers my head
anna sings and five notes deeper
sing the sisters there is this voice

behind all the others on the horse's back when
you click your toes when you bite
the last piece off the apple core along with
all the seeds when on the candelabra
everything goes out when the knit pricks
your ears these two clicks are
the flash

Notes on Contributors

MARTA AGUDO lives in Madrid. Her most recent collection, *Historial* (Valencia: Calambur, 2017), from which the poems in this issue are drawn, was named one of the best poetry volumes of the year by the Spanish critics.

CHARLOTTE BALDWIN is an arts programmer, creative writing tutor & dogwalker. As Gypsy Rose Poetry, she has performed everywhere from the National Poetry Library to nursing homes. Her work has appeared in a number of journals. In 2019, her poems appeared in *Islands Are But Mountains* (Platypus Press).

LINDA BLACK has three volumes from Shearsman Books, with a fourth currently in development. She is co-editor of *Long Poem Magazine*, and lives in London.

MELISSA BUCKHEIT is a queer poet, translator, activist, dancer and choreographer, photographer, English Lecturer and Orthopaedic Massage Therapist. She is the author of *Noctilucent* (Shearsman Books, 2012), and two chapbooks: *Dulcet You* (dancing girl press, 2016), and *Arc* (The Drunken Boat, 2007). She also translates the poet Ioulita Iliopoulou from Modern Greek, and currently lives in rural Northeast Connecticut.

SUSAN CONNOLLY has two full collections, including *Bridge of the Ford* (2016), and two chapbooks from Shearsman. Her most recent publication *What Noise on Earth* (Redfoxpress, 2019) is part of the C'est mon Dada collection of artists' books from visual poets around the world. She lives in Drogheda, Ireland.

HANNAH COOPER-SMITHSON IS currently completing a critical-creative PhD at Nottingham Trent University, where she is researching form in contemporary environmental poetry. Her work has appeared in various journals and anthologies, including *The Interpreters House, Finished Creatures, Anthropocene*, and *becoming-Botanical*, which was published by Objet-a Studios in 2019.

CLAIRE CROWTHER's most recent collection is *Solar Cruise* (Shearsman Books, 2020). She lives in Somerset and is co-editor of *Long Poem Magazine*.

AMY CRUTCHFIELD lives in Melbourne. She has had work published in *Australian Poetry Journal* and *Poetry Review*, amongst others.

KJELL ESPMARK is a Swedish poet with a long and illustrious career, and over 30 books to his name. Shearsman Books published his *Béla Bartók Against the Third Reich* in 1985, a joint publication with Oasis Books. The first three poems here are from *Evening's Freedom* (2019), a group of twenty poems exploring various examples of "late style" in artists. *A Cloud of Witnesses* (2020) is the third volume in a trilogy; the title alludes to *Hebrews* 12.i.

JANE FRANK is a poet from Brisbane. She is Director of the Centre for Creative Industries at Griffith University where she teaches creative and professional writing and literary studies. Her most recent chapbook is *Wide River* (Calanthe Press, 2020).

AMLANJYOTI GOSWAMI lives in New Delhi. His first collection, *River Wedding*, was published by Poetrywala, Mumbai, in 2019.

CHRISTOPHER GUTKIND is an Anglo-Canadian librarian in London, whose collection *Inside to Outside* was published by Shearsman Books in 2006. Poems from this sequence, *Digits After Orph*, are in *Otoliths* and *Erotoplasty* and *Berfrois*, and different poems will soon be in *Pamenar*.

DAVID HADBAWNIK's spectacular – and transgressive – version of the first six books of Virgil's *Aeneid* was published by Shearsman Books in 2015. Books 7–12 will follow in July 2021 in both hardcover and paperback editions. After some time teaching in Kuwait, he is now at the University of Wisconsin-Eau Claire in the U.S.A.

MANDY HAGGITH lives on a croft in Assynt, in the north-west highlands of Scotland and is a lecturer in literature and creative writing at the University of the Highlands and Islands. Her most recent book is *Why the Sky Is Far Away* (Red Squirrel Press, 2019). She has also written five novels, including a historical trilogy.

DAVID HACKBRIDGE JOHNSON is a composer and musician based in London. Three CDs of his orchestral music are available from Toccata Classics.

JEREMY HOOKER's *Selected Poems 1965–2018* and his essay collection, *Art of Seeing*, were published by Shearsman Books in 2020.

NORMAN JOPE is based in Plymouth and has collections from Shearsman (*Dreams of the Caucasus*, 2010), Waterloo Press, Stride and Knives, Forks and Spoons Press.

L. KIEW is a Chinese Malaysian poet from London, where she works as an accountant. Her debut pamphlet, *The Unquiet*, was published by Offord Road Books in 2019. She was longlisted in the 2019 National Poetry Competition.

PETER LARKIN has a number of books from Shearsman, most recently *Encroach to Resume* (2021), and *Trees Before Abstinent Ground* (2019).

MARY LEADER has two collections from Shearsman Books, with a third, *Distaff*, in development. She lives in Oklahoma.

CAROLA LUTHER has two collections with Carcanet Press, with a third coming this year. She has mostly worked as a therapeutic counsellor, but has also taught poetry part-time at Manchester Metropolitan University and Liverpool John Moores University.

ROBIN FULTON MACPHERSON is a Scottish poet living for several decades in Norway, whose most recent collection, *Arrivals of Light*, was published by Shearsman Books in 2020. His *Collected Poems* appeared from Marick Press in the U.S.A. in 2013. He has also translated many Swedish and Norwegian poets, including Kjell Espmark, Gunnar Harding and Tomas Tranströmer.

OLIVIA McCANNON's collection *Exactly My Own Length* (Carcanet/Oxford Poets) was shortlisted for the Seamus Heaney Centre Prize and won the Fenton Aldeburgh First Collection Prize. She lived for nine years in Paris, and her translations from French run from Renaissance to contemporary poetry as well as Balzac's novel *Old Man Goriot* for Penguin Classics (2011).

PETER ROBINSON teaches at the University of Reading and is poetry editor for Two Rivers Press. Shearsman Books has published, among many other volumes, his *Collected Poems 1976–2016*. *The Personal Art: Essays, Reviews & Memoirs* will appear in

2021, as will *Peter Robinson: A Portrait of his Work*, edited by Tom Phillips.

DAVID RUSHMER's first full collection, *Remains to Be Seen*, was published by Shearsman Books in 2018.

ANNIE RUTHERFORD is Programme Co-ordinator at StAnza. Her translation of Swiss/German poet Nora Gomringer appeared in 2018 with Burning Eye Books, and her translation of Belarusian poet Volha Hapeyeva will appear from Arc during 2021.

LAWRENCE SCHIMEL is an American writer, translator and publisher, based in Madrid. Shearsman has published his translations of Jordi Doce and Elsa Cross.

MAURICE SCULLY's one-volume collected *Things That Happen* project, written over a period of 25 years, was published by Shearsman Books in 2020, alongside a volume of essays on his work, edited by Kenneth Keating. His next book will appear in 2022.

AIDAN SEMMENS has four collection from Shearsman Books, most recently *There Will Be Singing* (2020). He edits the online magazine, *Molly Bloom*.

LUCY SHEERMAN runs the University of Cambridge Centre for Creative Writing. Publications include: *Rarefied* (Oystercatcher) and *Fragments Salvaged from her Diary* (Dancing Girl Press).

AGNIESZKA STUDZIŃSKA has an MA in Creative Writing from the UEA and two full collections, *Snow Calling* (Salt, 2010) and *What Things Are* (Eyewear, 2014). She is currently working on a PhD at Royal Holloway and lives in London. Shearsman Books will publish her third collection, *Branches of a House*, later in 2021.

SCOTT THURSTON is based in Manchester and teaches at Salford University. His Shearsman publications include *Internal Rhyme* (2010), and a volume of interviews with women poets, *Talking Poetics* (2011).

KINGA TÓTH is a writer, and a visual and sound poet, working in Hungarian, German and English. She has performed and exhibited her work internationally. In 2018–2019 she was the City Writer in Graz. Her collection *We Build A City*, translated into English by Sven Engelke and the author, appeared with Knives Forks and Spoons Press in 2020.

ANANNYA UBEROI is a full-time software engineer and part-time tea connoisseur based in Madrid. She is poetry editor at *The Bookends Review*, and the winner of the 6th Singapore Poetry Contest. Her work has appeared in a number of journals and her website is www.anannyauberoi.com.

VIRGIL (70–19 BC) was the national poet of Imperial Rome, and his *Aeneid* – an epic on the founding of Rome – is one of the great monuments of early Western literature.

Nearly all of **JOHN WELCH**'s work is published by Shearsman Books, including a *Collected Poems* (2008), *In Folly's Shade* (2018) and a memoir, *Dreaming Arrival* (2008).

PETRA WHITE is an Australian poet, now living in Berlin. Her most recent collection is *Reading for a Quiet Morning* (Gloria SMH Press, 2017).

TAMAR YOSELOFF's sixth collection is *The Black Place* (Seren, 2019). She is also the author of *Formerly* (with photographs by Vici MacDonald), and collaborative editions with artists Linda Karshan and Charlotte Harker respectively, and lectures on the Poetry School / Newcastle University MA in Writing Poetry.

Lightning Source UK Ltd.
Milton Keynes UK
UKHW010743060421
381518UK00001B/123